W9-DIH-873

RESEARCH TOOLS YOU CAN USE

How Do I Use a Dictionary?

Jennifer Landau

Britannica®
Educational Publishing

IN ASSOCIATION WITH

ROSEN
EDUCATIONAL SERVICES

Published in 2015 by Britannica Educational Publishing (a trademark of Encyclopædia Britannica, Inc.) in association with The Rosen Publishing Group, Inc.
29 East 21st Street, New York, NY 10010

Distributed exclusively by Rosen Publishing.
To see additional Britannica Educational Publishing titles, go to rosenpublishing.com.

First Edition

Britannica Educational Publishing
J.E. Luebering: Director, Core Reference Group
Mary Rose McCudden: Editor, Britannica Student Encyclopedia

Rosen Publishing
Hope Lourie Killcoyne: Executive Editor
Kathy Kuhtz Campbell: Editor
Nelson Sá: Art Director
Brian Garvey: Designer
Cindy Reiman: Photography Manager
Marty Levick: Photo Researcher

Cataloging-in-Publication Data

Landau, Jennifer, 1961–
How do I use a dictionary?/Jennifer Landau.—First Edition.
     pages cm.—(Research tools you can use)
Includes bibliographical references and index.
Audience: Grades 3–6.
ISBN 978-1-62275-344-4 (library bound)—ISBN 978-1-62275-345-1 (pbk.)—ISBN 978-1-62275-368-0 (6-pack)
1. English language—Dictionaries—Juvenile literature. 2. Encyclopedias and dictionaries—Juvenile literature. I. Title.
PE1611.L36 2015
423.028—dc23
                                                                                        2014002033

Manufactured in the United States of America

Photo credits: Cover and interior pages (background) © iStockphoto.com/Blue Army; cover (inset from left) YanLev/Shutterstock.com, lightpoet/Shutterstock.com, SnowWhiteimages/Shutterstock.com; p. 4 © AP Images; pp. 5, 6 (left), 13, 14, 23 By permission. From Merriam-Webster's Elementary Dictionary © 2014 by Merriam-Webster, Inc. (www.Merriam-Webster.com); p. 6 (right) British Library/Robana/Hulton Fine Art Collection/Getty Images; p. 7 Library of Congress Prints and Photographs Division; pp. 8–9 Jon Feingersh/Blend Images/Getty Images; p. 9 © North Wind Picture Archives; p. 10 Private Collection/© Look and Learn/Elgar Collection/The Bridgeman Art Library; p. 11 Lim Yong Hian/Shutterstock.com; p. 15 Yu Lan/Shutterstock.com; pp. 16–17 iofoto/Shutterstock.com (web page in monitor © 2014 Dictionary.com, LLC. All Rights Reserved); p. 19 © Merriam-Webster, Inc.; p. 21 Christopher Ewing/iStock/Thinkstock; pp. 26–27 mocker_bat/iStock/Thinkstock; p. 28 Isac Goufart/iStock/Thinkstock.

CONTENTS

CHAPTER 1

What Is a Dictionary?

There are dictionaries available for all age groups and reading levels.

A dictionary is a book that lists words and gives their meanings. English-language dictionaries list the words from "A" to "Z," which is known as alphabetical order. A dictionary shows you how to use a word in a sentence. Dictionaries provide other information, too. The word is spelled correctly and divided into syllables. It is also marked to show how to **pronounce** it the right way.

Dictionaries let a student know whether a word is a noun, verb, adjective, or another part of speech. In many dictionaries, synonyms and antonyms for words are given. Synonyms are words that mean the same as the word you are looking up, while antonyms have the opposite meaning. Many dictionaries include drawings to help you understand what a word means. Good dictionaries are available for all ages and reading levels.

ter·ri·er \'ter-ē-ər\ *n* : a usually small dog originally used by hunters to force animals from their holes

word history

terrier

Terriers were first used in hunting. Their job was to dig for small animals and force them from their holes. The word **terrier** comes from a medieval French phrase *chen terrer* (or *chien terrier*), literally, "earth dog." The *terr-* in *terrier* comes ultimately from Latin *terra*, "earth."

Some dictionaries provide the history of a word to show how it became part of the language.

Pronounce means to make the proper sound of a letter or word.

The earliest dictionaries were put together to explain difficult words and words in a foreign language, meaning a language spoken in a different country. Easy words were not included because it was felt that everyone knew them. Today, it is the words that are used most often that are likely to end up in a dictionary.

keyhole • killer

ment with a row of keys like that of a piano **3** : the whole arrangement of keys (as on a computer or typewriter)
key·hole \ˈkē-ˌhōl\ *n* : a hole for receiving a key
key·note \ˈkē-ˌnōt\ *n* **1** : the first tone of a scale fundamental to harmony **2** : the fundamental fact, idea, or mood
key·stone \ˈkē-ˌstōn\ *n* **1** : the wedge-shaped piece at the top of an arch that locks the other pieces in place **2** : something on which other things depend for support

keystone

keystone 1

Drawings can help give you a better understanding of a word's meaning.

WORD WORKERS

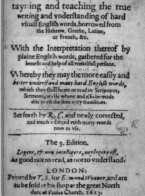

The first English-language dictionary was Robert Cawdrey's *A Table Alphabeticall*, published in 1604. It was little more than a list of words in Latin and French.

What Is a Dictionary?

Noah Webster was born in 1758. He worked as a teacher, lawyer, editor, and judge. In 1828, he produced the first great American dictionary. *An American Dictionary of the English Language* included about seventy

It took Noah Webster twenty-two years to complete *An American Dictionary of the English Language.*

thousand words. It showed how words in the United States often had a different meaning from the same words as they were used in England.

CHAPTER 2

Different Types of Dictionaries

There are many different types of dictionaries. An abridged dictionary is a smaller dictionary that contains words that people use most often. An unabridged dictionary has no

An unabridged dictionary is a complete dictionary. It has not been shortened by leaving out terms or definitions.

word limit and can contain hundreds of thousands of words. *The Oxford English Dictionary (OED)* is the most well-known unabridged dictionary. It was first released, under a different title, in 10 separate volumes, published between 1884 and 1928.

The editors of the *OED* try to keep the dictionary up to date. If you go

WORD WORKERS

Englishman Samuel Johnson published *A Dictionary of the English Language* in 1755. It is thought of as the first modern dictionary and was the most well-known English-language dictionary until the *OED* was published over a hundred years later.

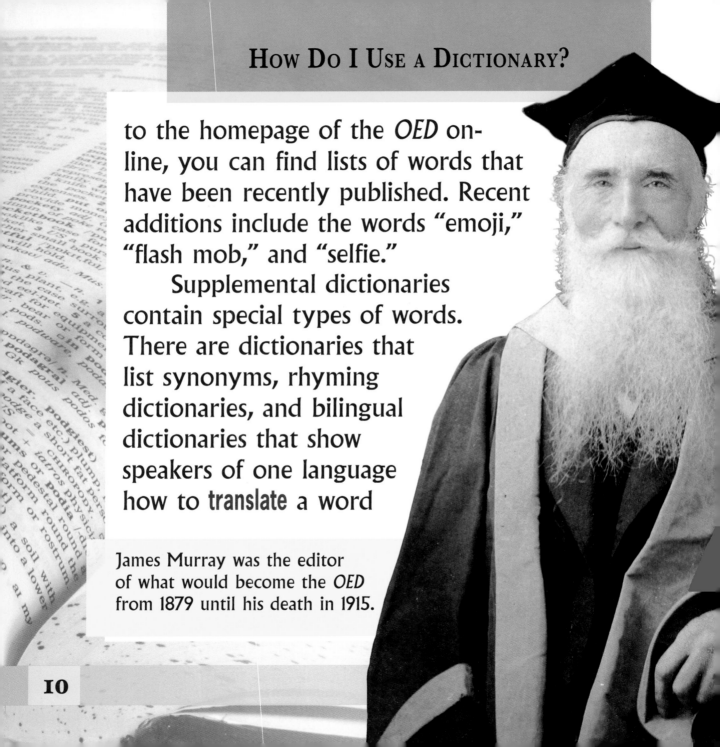

to the homepage of the *OED* on-line, you can find lists of words that have been recently published. Recent additions include the words "emoji," "flash mob," and "selfie."

Supplemental dictionaries contain special types of words. There are dictionaries that list synonyms, rhyming dictionaries, and bilingual dictionaries that show speakers of one language how to **translate** a word

James Murray was the editor of what would become the *OED* from 1879 until his death in 1915.

into another language.

Many free online dictionaries are available. These dictionaries offer much of the same information as print dictionaries. One advantage of an online dictionary is that you can click on a word and listen to its pronunciation.

This Chinese-English dictionary shows how to translate Chinese characters into English words.

Translate means to change a word from one language into another.

CHAPTER 3

The Importance of Alphabetical Order

The best place to start when using an English-language dictionary is the first few pages. Every dictionary has a guide that shows how to use it, and looking over this information can save time and energy. Online dictionaries have similar information in the help section or elsewhere on their website.

A dictionary is divided by letter, beginning with "A" and ending with "Z." Each letter has lists of words set in boldface just outside the margin of the page. These are called entry words.

Main Entry Words

When you open your dictionary to just about any page, you will find a list of words down the left-hand column printed in heavy black **boldface** type. Each of these is followed by information that explains or tells something about the word. The boldface word or phrase together with the explanation is a **dictionary entry,** and the boldface word itself is the **entry word** or **main entry.**

s \\'es\\ *n, pl* **s's** *or* **ss** \\'e-səz\\ *often cap*   **1** : the 19th letter of the English alphabet   **2** : a grade rating a student's work as satisfactory
³-s *vb suffix* — used to form the third person singular present of most verbs that do not end in *s, z, sh, ch, x,* or *y* following a consonant ⟨fall*s*⟩ ⟨take*s*⟩ ⟨play*s*⟩
saber–toothed tiger *n* : a very large extinct cat of prehistoric times with long sharp curved upper canine teeth
²safe *n* : a metal box with a lock that is used for keeping something (as money) safe

Each dictionary has pages at the beginning to explain how to use it. Entry words in the dictionary are set in boldface type.

Entry words are listed in alphabetical order. This means that every word that begins with "A" comes before every word that begins with "B," and every word beginning with "B" comes before all the "C" words. This pattern continues throughout the dictionary. The same idea holds true within each letter of the alphabet. For example, "again" is listed before "apple" because "g" comes before "p" in the alphabet.

Most dictionaries have a pair of guide words written at the top of every page. Following in

duel • duplicate

²**duel** *vb* **du·eled** *or* **du·elled; du·el·ing** *or* **ling** : to take part in an agreed-upon fight weapons

du·et \dü-ˈet, dyü-\ *n* **1** : a piece of music for two performers **2** : two people performing music together

dug *past and past participle of* DIG

dug·out \ˈdəg-ˌaút\ *n* **1** : a low shelter facing a baseball diamond and containing the players' bench **2** : a shelter dug in a hillside or in the ground **3** : a

a
b
c
d
e
f
g
h

Guide words at the top of a page show you the first and last entry words on that page.

alphabetical order, these are the first and last words listed on that page. If you are trying to find a certain word, guide words can help you move through the dictionary more quickly. Not every dictionary has the same guide words at the top, but these words are always listed in alphabetical order.

Some dictionaries have thumb cuts that are marked with letters of the alphabet in the edge of pages. These marks make it easy to turn to a certain part.

By looking at the two guide words, you can figure out if the word you are searching for falls between them. For example, the word "partner" falls between "particular" and "passing," so that would be the page that you would check.

If you have no idea how to spell a word, do your best to sound out the first couple of letters. Then use the guide words to help you narrow it

down. If you really get stuck, you can ask an adult to help you get started.

Browse means to read or look over something in a light or careless way.

Although online dictionaries do not have guide words at the top of the page, when you **browse** by letter you will see a listing of words arranged in alphabetical order, just like in a print dictionary.

When you use an online dictionary, you can click on a word to hear how it is pronounced.

17

CHAPTER 4

Getting the Most Out of Your Dictionary

Once you find your entry word based on alphabetical order, the dictionary has a lot of information to offer beyond the correct spelling. Next to the entry word is its pronunciation, which shows you how to sound out a word. The pronunciation of a word is set off in parentheses or brackets. The first few pages of the dictionary will explain what the different pronunciation symbols mean. There may be also a shorter pronunciation guide at the bottom of each page.

These dictionary symbols might seem strange at first, but they are a big help when figuring out

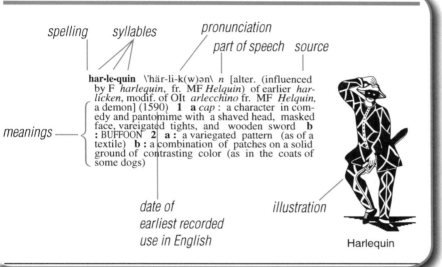

spelling syllables pronunciation part of speech source

har·le·quin \'här-li-k(w)ən\ *n* [alter. (influenced by F *harlequin*, fr. MF *Helquin*) of earlier *har-licken*, modif. of OIt *arlecchino* fr. MF *Helquin*, a demon] (1590) **1 a** *cap* : a character in comedy and pantomime with a shaved head, masked face, variegated tights, and wooden sword **b** : BUFFOON **2 a :** a variegated pattern (as of a textile) **b :** a combination of patches on a solid ground of contrasting color (as in the coats of some dogs)

meanings

date of earliest recorded use in English

illustration

Harlequin

A dictionary entry contains the entry word along with information about that word.

how to say a word. Online dictionaries and dictionary apps provide these symbols, too. They also give you a chance to hear the word pronounced properly.

Within the brackets or parentheses, you'll also see how to divide the word into syllables. A syllable is a unit of spoken language. Depending on which dictionary you are using, syllable divisions will be shown by dots, dashes, or space breaks. In the word "partner," for example, the syllable break is set between "part" and "ner."

Accent marks point out which syllable is stressed in the word. In dictionary terms, stress means which syllable gets spoken with more force. In "partner," the accent mark is placed over the first syllable "part" because it is pronounced more forcefully.

After the pronunciation, you will see an **abbreviation** that tells you how the entry word is used in a sentence. This is called its part of speech.

Words used to name a person, place, or thing ("part-ner," "California," "apple") are

Abbreviation means a shortened form of a word that is used in place of the entire word.

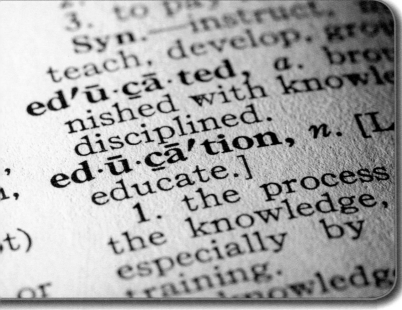

With the help of pronunciation symbols, you can learn how to pronounce any word in the dictionary.

called nouns. The letter "n" is the abbreviation for "noun."

Words that show an action or state of being ("laugh," "jump," "live") are called verbs. The letters "vb" are the abbreviation for "verb."

Words used to describe something about a noun ("green," "pretty," "upsetting") are called adjectives. The letters "adj" are the abbreviation for "adjective."

Words that point out where, when, or how something happened ("there," "tomorrow," "slowly") are called adverbs. The letters "adv" are the abbreviation for "adverb."

Words that link different parts of a sentence ("yet," "but," "and") are called conjunctions. The letters "conj" are the abbreviation for conjunction.

The definition of a word explains its meaning. If there is more than one meaning, the most basic definition is listed first. In *Webster's Elementary Dictionary*, for example, the first definition of "partner," marked with the number 1, is "a person who does or shares something with another."

The entry word is then used in a sentence: "You are my favorite dancing *partner.*" The second definition (2) is "either one of a married couple."

Signs and Symbols

ASTRONOMY

☉	the sun; Sunday	♂	Mars; Tuesday
☾, or ☽	the moon; Monday	♃	Jupiter; Thursday
●	new moon	♄	Saturn; Saturday
☽, or ☾	first quarter	♅	Uranus
○	full moon	♆	Neptune
☾, or ☾	last quarter	♇	Pluto
☿	Mercury; Wednesday	☄	comet
♀	Venus; Friday	✴ or ✳	fixed star
⊕ or ♁	Earth		

BUSINESS

@	at; each ⟨4 apples @ 5¢ = 20¢⟩	‰	per thousand
c/o	care of	$	dollars
#	number if it precedes a numeral ⟨track #3⟩; pounds if it follows ⟨a 5# sack of sugar⟩	¢	cents
		£	pounds
		©	copyrighted
℔	pound; pounds	®	registered trademark
%	percent		

COMPUTERS

?	symbol used especially to represent any single character in a search of a file or database (as in a search for "f?n" to find *fan*, *fin*, and *fun*)	@	at sign—used to introduce the domain name in an e-mail address
*	symbol used especially to represent zero or more characters in a search of a file or database (as in a search for "key*" to find *key*, *keys*, *keyed*, *keying*, etc.)	/ or \	—used to introduce or separate parts of a computer address
		.	dot—used to separate parts of a computer address or file name

MATHEMATICS

+	plus; positive ⟨$a + b = c$⟩	×	multiplied by; times ⟨$6 \times 4 = 24$⟩ — also indicated by placing a dot between the factors ⟨$6 \cdot 4 = 24$⟩
−	minus; negative		
±	plus or minus ⟨the square root of $4a^2$ is $\pm 2a$⟩		

The final two definitions for this entry word are (3) "someone who plays with another person on the same side in a game" and (4) "one of two or more people who run a business together."

Other parts of a dictionary

Many dictionaries provide maps, scientific symbols, and other types of information at the back of the book.

include the foreign-language roots of certain words, meaning how they can be traced back to another language. Items such as maps, writer's guides, and weights and measures can often be found at the back of a dictionary.

Once you know how to use a dictionary, it will be a great reference for years to come. You'll understand the English language on a deeper level and be able to spell, read, and write with more confidence.

CHAPTER 5

Practice Your Dictionary Skills

1. Put the words in each list in alphabetical order:

FLOOD
FAMOUS
FAMILIAR
FLAVOR
FASHION

PLATTER
PARTNER
PARDON
PLENTY
PLEASANT

2. Use guide words to find the words listed below in your dictionary. Write those guide words down on paper. The answers could be different depending on which dictionary is used.

ASLEEP

LUMP

EXIT

POTATO

SEASON

3. Use a dictionary to divide the following words into syllables. Rewrite the words with a dot between each syllable.

DEPARTMENT

UNFORTUNATE

HAMBURGER

WOBBLY

NECESSARY

After you have mastered the use of a dictionary, try to learn new words. Open up the dictionary, pick a word that is new to you, and read about it. Try to use that word later.

4. Use a dictionary to label the parts of speech for each word below. Remember: some words can be used as more than one part of speech.

FLOWER

BECAUSE

MACHINE

MOP

UGLY

YET

When you look up new words, try to remember how they are used in sentences so that you can use them correctly down the road.

5. Find each word in the dictionary. Pick the correct meaning from the three choices below.

BROOD

a) a hiding place
b) a group of birds hatched at the same time
c) a large cape

TIMID

a) patient
b) excitable
c) shy

FULFILL

a) to satisfy
b) to measure out the correct amount of something
c) to move at a fast pace

SCARCE

a) shocking
b) few in number
c) easy to find

antonyms Words of opposite meaning.

bilingual Using or expressed in two languages.

boldface A heavy black type.

confidence A feeling of certainty.

editors People whose jobs involve reading and correcting pieces of writing so that they can be published or used.

foreign Belonging to a different place or country.

lawyer A person whose job is to guide others in matters of the law.

margin The part of a page or sheet outside the main body of print or writing.

parentheses Upright, curved lines used to enclose words or figures.

published Prepared and produced for sale, such as a book, magazine, or newspaper.

reference A source of information.

symbols Letters, groups of letters, characters, or pictures that are used to stand for something else.

synonyms Words having the same or almost the same meaning.

BOOKS

American Heritage Children's Dictionary. Boston, MA: Houghton Mifflin Harcourt, 2012.

DK Publishing. *Children's Illustrated Dictionary*. New York, NY: Dorling Kindersley Ltd., 2009.

Merriam–Webster's Elementary Dictionary. Updated and expanded ed. Springfield, MA: Merriam-Webster, Inc., 2014.

Scholastic Children's Dictionary. New York, NY: Scholastic, 2013.

WEBSITES

Because of the changing nature of Internet links, Rosen Publishing has developed an online list of websites related to the subject of this book. This site is updated regularly. Please use this link to access the list:

http://www.rosenlinks.com/RTYCU/Dict

Index